HAL LEONARD

UKULELE METHOD

UKULELE FOR KIDS

A Beginner's Guide with Step-by-Step Instruction for Ukulele

BY CHAD JOHNSON

Ukuleles featured in this book courtesy of Lanikai Ukulele

T0079542

To access audio visit:
www.halleonard.com/mylibrary

Enter Code
4691-8521-7866-2579

ISBN 978-1-61774-239-2

7777 W. BLUEMOUND RD. P.O. BOX 13819 MILWAUKEE, WI 53213

Visit Hal Leonard Online at
www.halleonard.com

SELECTING YOUR UKULELE

Ukuleles mainly come in four sizes:

Soprano (or "standard") Concert Tenor Baritone

Even a baritone ukulele isn't very big, but the soprano, concert, or tenor is probably best for a child to learn on. Pick the one that feels best to you.

Too Big Good Fit

PARTS OF THE UKULELE

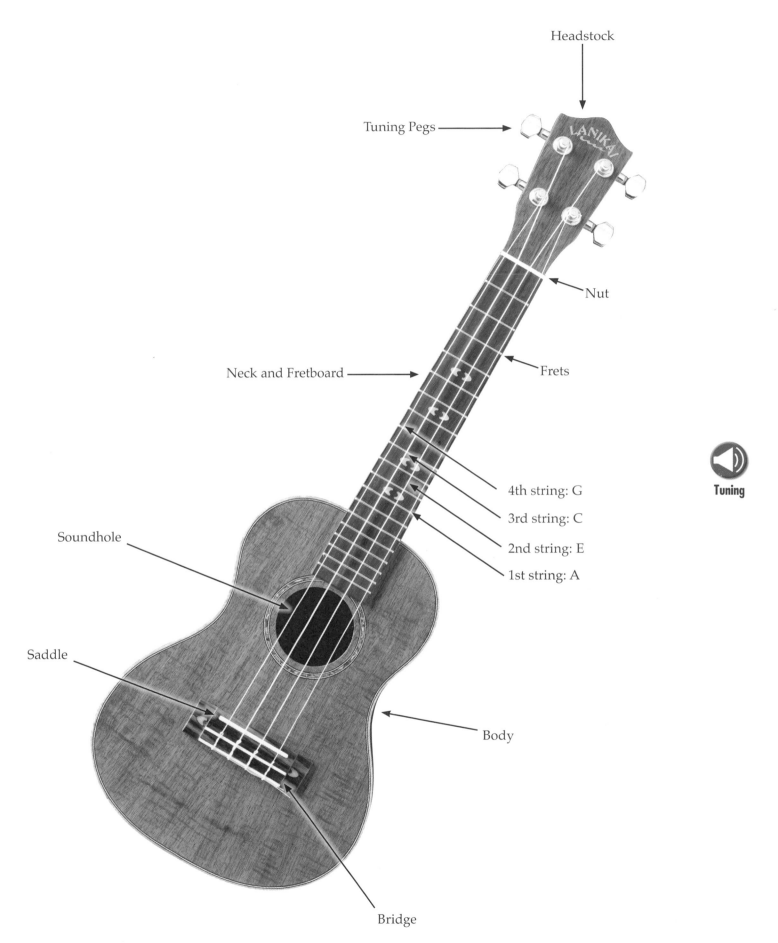

Headstock

Tuning Pegs

Nut

Neck and Fretboard

Frets

4th string: G

3rd string: C

2nd string: E

1st string: A

Soundhole

Saddle

Body

Bridge

Tuning

HOLDING THE UKULELE

There are many ways to hold a ukulele, both sitting and standing.

Sitting

- Sit up straight and relax your shoulders
- Place your feet flat on the floor or place one foot on a foot stool
- Tilt the neck of the ukulele slightly upwards
- Rest the ukulele on your leg or keep it in place by cradling it with your arm against your body

Wearing a Strap

Alternatively, you can wear a strap to keep your ukulele in place (sitting or standing). This will also allow the instrument to vibrate more freely and generally produce a bigger sound.

Standing

- Cradle the ukulele under the strumming arm to keep it in place
- Don't squeeze too tightly
- Tilt the neck of the ukulele slightly upwards

HAND POSITION

Left Hand

The fingers are numbered 1 through 4 (thumb is not numbered). Press the string down firmly between the two frets.

Place your thumb in the middle of the back of the neck and arch your fingers so that your palm doesn't touch the neck.

Right Hand

There are several ways to pluck or strum the strings of the ukulele. Most people strum the strings with either their extended first finger or thumb.

Some people prefer to play with a pick. Hold the pick between your thumb and first finger as shown in the photo and concentrating on using a downstroke to pick one string at a time.

THE C CHORD

Most people use the ukulele to play chords while they sing along. A **chord** is sounded when more than two strings are played at the same time. To play your first chord, C, use your 3rd finger to press the 3rd fret at the 1st string.

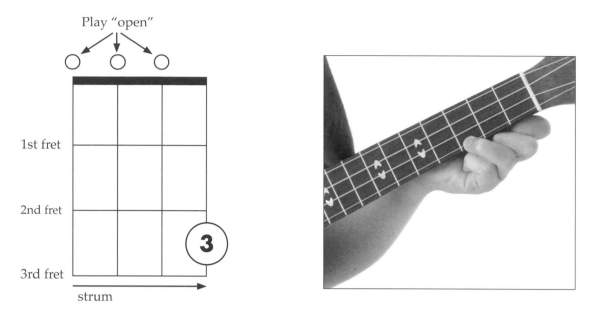

Music has a steady **beat**, like the ticking of a clock. Count aloud as you strum.

strum	strum	strum	strum	strum	strum	strum	strum
/	/	/	/	/	/	/	/
1	2	3	4	1	2	3	4

ARE YOU STRUMMING 🔊

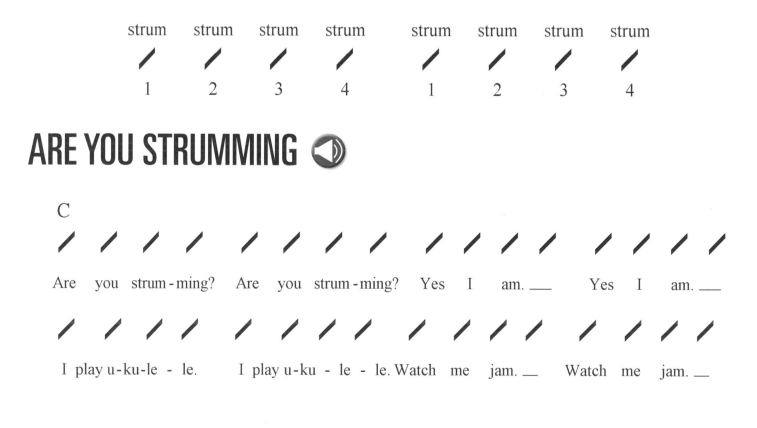

C

/ / / /   / / / /   / / / /   / / / /

Are you strum-ming?   Are you strum-ming? Yes I am. ___   Yes I am. ___

/ / / /   / / / /   / / / /   / / / /

I play u-ku-le - le.   I play u-ku - le - le. Watch me jam. ___   Watch me jam. ___

TEACHER MELODY:

THE F CHORD

For the F chord, we'll use two fingers. Use your 2nd finger to press the 4th string at the 2nd fret, and use your 1st finger to press the 2nd string at the 1st fret.

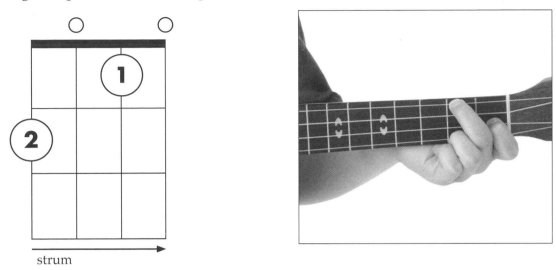

strum

Bar lines divide music into **measures**. A **double bar line** means the end.

Measure — Measure

Bar line · Double bar line

STRUM THE UKE

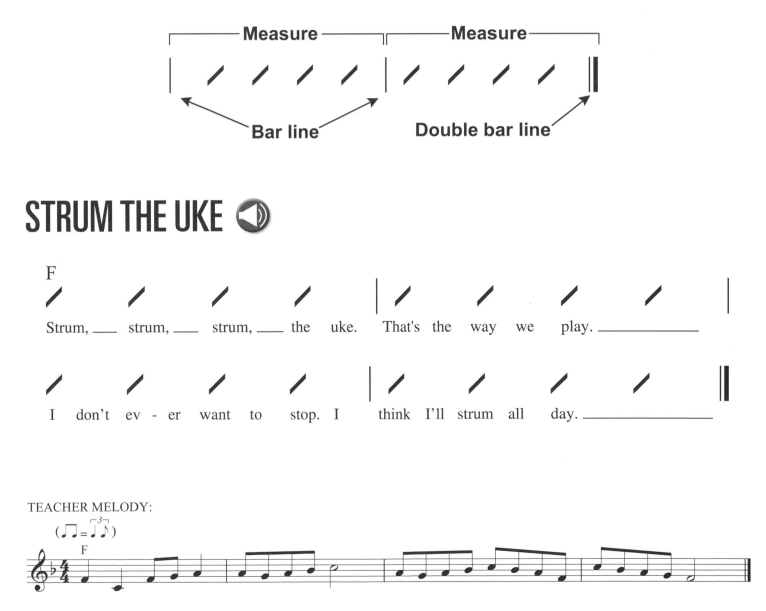

F

Strum, ___ strum, ___ strum, ___ the uke. That's the way we play. _____

I don't ev - er want to stop. I think I'll strum all day. _____

TEACHER MELODY:

CHANGING CHORDS

Practice strumming the F chord, and then change to the C chord.

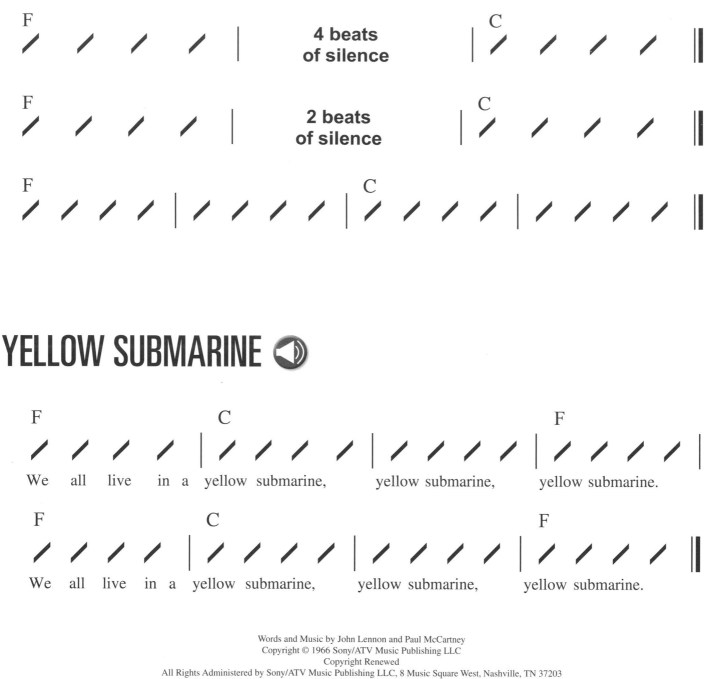

YELLOW SUBMARINE

We all live in a yellow submarine, yellow submarine, yellow submarine.

We all live in a yellow submarine, yellow submarine, yellow submarine.

Words and Music by John Lennon and Paul McCartney
Copyright © 1966 Sony/ATV Music Publishing LLC
Copyright Renewed
All Rights Administered by Sony/ATV Music Publishing LLC, 8 Music Square West, Nashville, TN 37203
International Copyright Secured   All Rights Reserved

TEACHER ACCOMPANIMENT:

THE C7 CHORD

We can change one note from our C chord to make a C7 chord. Use your 1st finger to press the 1st string at the 1st fret.

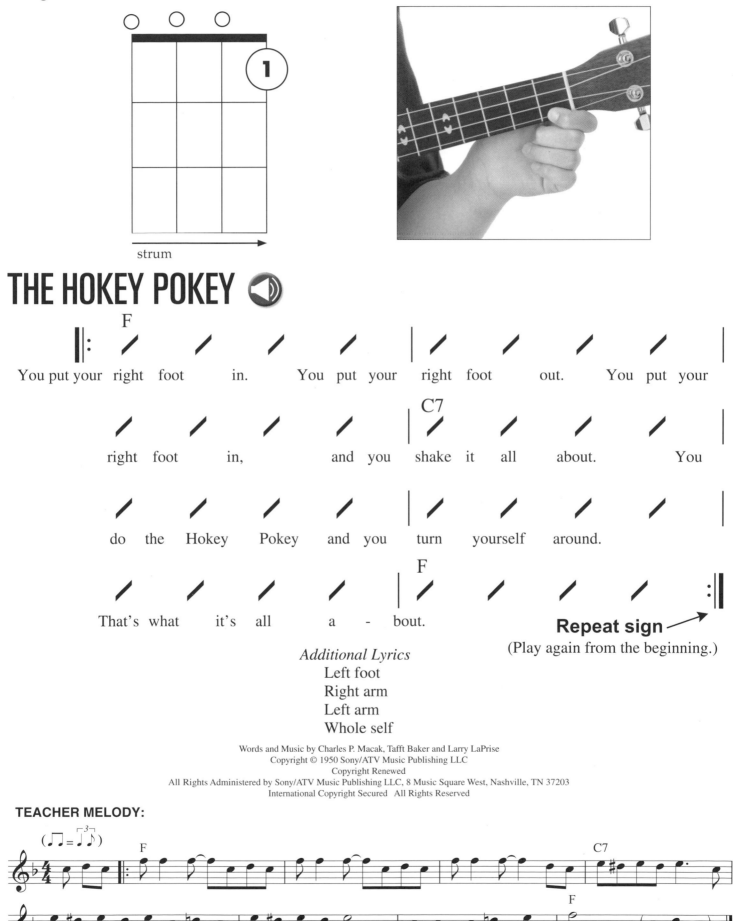

strum

THE HOKEY POKEY

F

‖: / / / / | / / / / |

You put your right foot in. You put your right foot out. You put your

/ / / / | **C7** / / / / |

right foot in, and you shake it all about. You

/ / / / | / / / / |

do the Hokey Pokey and you turn yourself around.

F

/ / / / | / / / / :‖

That's what it's all a - bout.

Repeat sign
(Play again from the beginning.)

Additional Lyrics
Left foot
Right arm
Left arm
Whole self

Words and Music by Charles P. Macak, Tafft Baker and Larry LaPrise
Copyright © 1950 Sony/ATV Music Publishing LLC
Copyright Renewed
All Rights Administered by Sony/ATV Music Publishing LLC, 8 Music Square West, Nashville, TN 37203
International Copyright Secured All Rights Reserved

TEACHER MELODY:

THE A MINOR CHORD

Use your 2nd finger to press the 4th string at the 2nd fret.

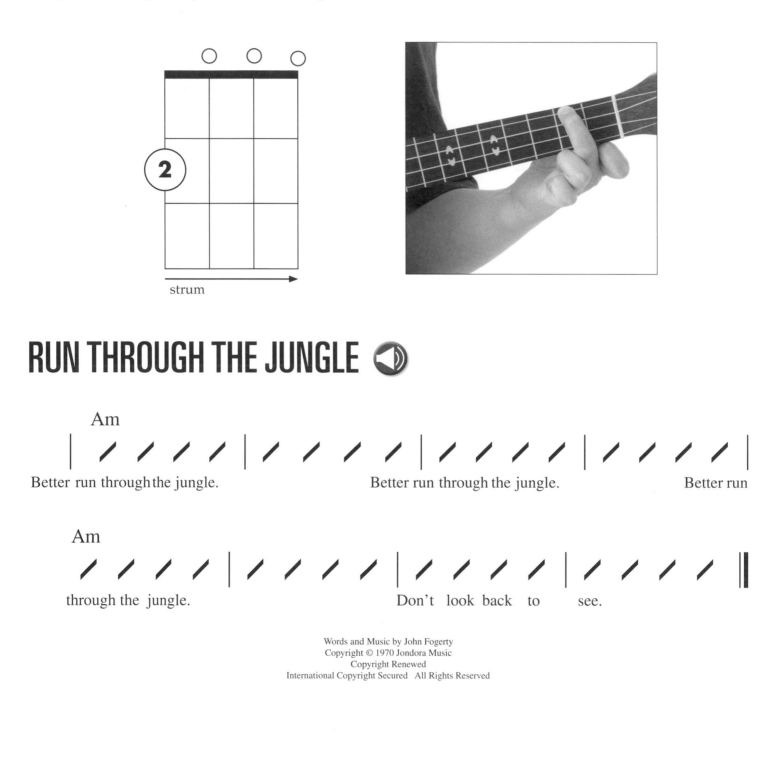

RUN THROUGH THE JUNGLE

Am

Better run through the jungle.　　　Better run through the jungle.　　　Better run

Am

through the jungle.　　　Don't look back to see.

TEACHER MELODY:

Am

Switching between Am and F is really easy. Try it out in this Beatles song.

ELEANOR RIGBY

F   Am

Ah, _____ look at all   the   lonely   people! _____

Am   F

Eleanor Rigby _____ picks up the rice   in the church   where a   wedding has been, _____

             Am

lives in a dream. _____ Waits at the window,   wearing the face that she keeps   in a jar   by the

F   Am

door, _____   who is it for? _____   All   the   lonely   people,   where

F   Am

do   they all   come from?   All   the   lonely   people,

                     F   Am

where   do   they all   be - long?

Words and Music by John Lennon and Paul McCartney
Copyright © 1966 Sony/ATV Music Publishing LLC
Copyright Renewed
All Rights Administered by Sony/ATV Music Publishing LLC, 8 Music Square West, Nashville, TN 37203
International Copyright Secured All Rights Reserved

TEACHER MELODY:

11

THE G CHORD

For the G chord, you'll press three notes at the same time.

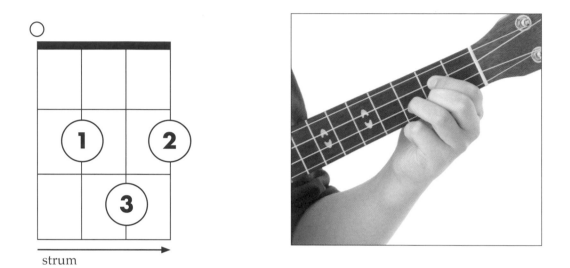

strum

Let's try changing between three chords you know.

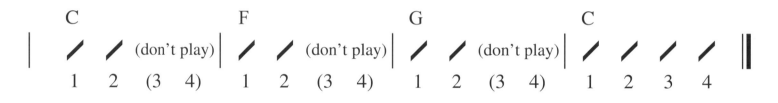

In this song, we'll be switching back and forth between G and F chords with no space in between.

WATCHIN' THE WAVES

TEACHER MELODY:

Now let's try our first songs with three different chords: C, F, and G.

THREE LITTLE BIRDS

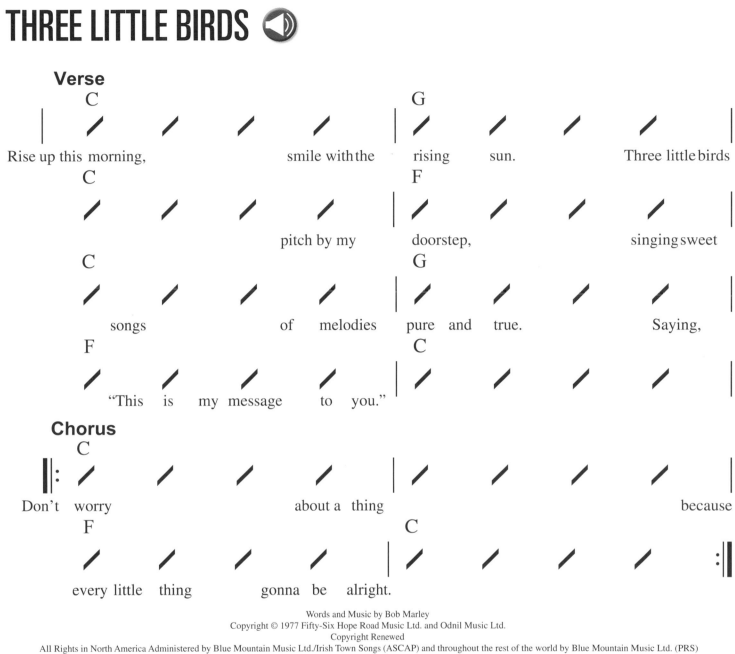

Verse

| C | | | | G | | | |
Rise up this morning, smile with the rising sun. Three little birds

| C | | | | F | | | |
pitch by my doorstep, singing sweet

| C | | | | G | | | |
songs of melodies pure and true. Saying,

| F | | | | C | | | |
"This is my message to you."

Chorus

| C | | | | | | | |
Don't worry about a thing because

| F | | | | C | | | |
every little thing gonna be alright.

TEACHER MELODY:

Chords sometimes change in the middle of a measure too. Watch out for that in this next classic song by the Temptations.

AIN'T TOO PROUD TO BEG

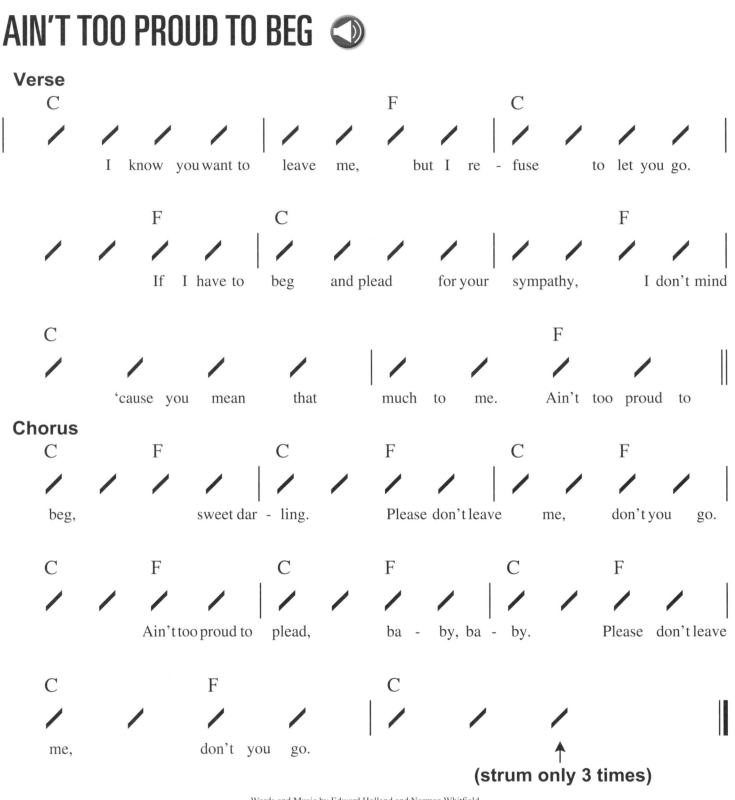

Words and Music by Edward Holland and Norman Whitfield
© 1966 (Renewed 1994) JOBETE MUSIC CO., INC.
All Rights Controlled and Administered by EMI BLACKWOOD MUSIC INC. on behalf of STONE AGATE MUSIC (A Division of JOBETE MUSIC CO., INC.)
All Rights Reserved   International Copyright Secured   Used by Permission

TEACHER MELODY:

THE NOTE A

So far, you have learned to play chords. If you remember, a chord is sounded when you play more than two strings together. Now let's play some single notes. This is the way we play melodies on the ukulele.

To play the A note, pluck the 1st string open with your finger, thumb, or pick.

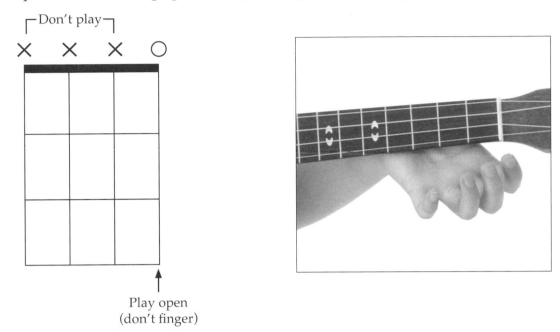

Music is written on a **staff** of five lines and four spaces. Each line or space is assigned a letter name. A **clef** appears at the beginning of every staff. Ukulele music is written on a **treble clef**.

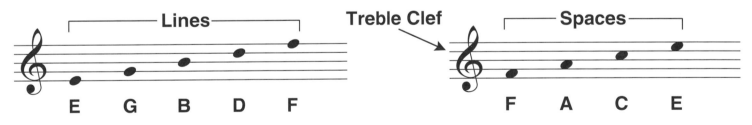

Our open 1st string is the note A, which is the second space up on the staff. Play each A note slowly and evenly.

MALAGUEÑA 🔊

TEACHER ACCOMPANIMENT:

THE NOTE B

Use your 2nd finger to press the 1st string at the 2nd fret.

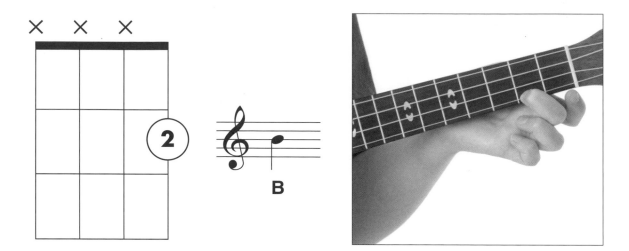

B

A **time signature** appears at the beginning of a piece of music. It tells how many beats are in each measure and what kind of note is counted as one beat. In 4/4 ("four-four") time, there are four beats in each measure, and a **quarter note** is counted as one beat. It has a solid notehead and a stem (♩).

TWO NOTE JAM

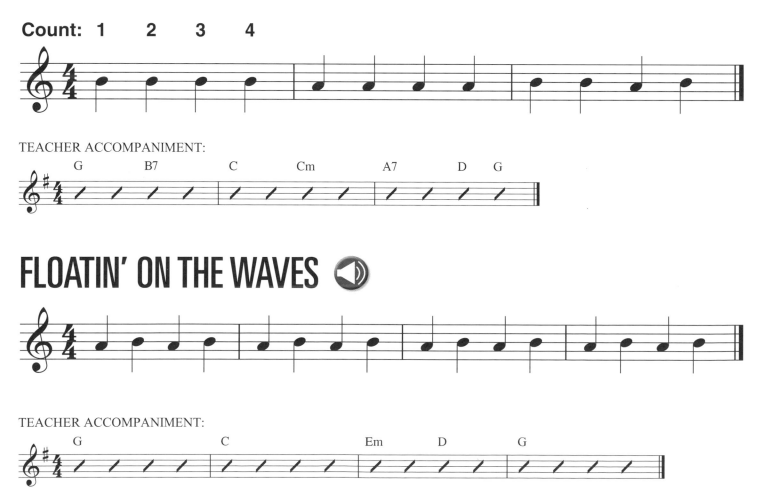

THE NOTE C

Use your 3rd finger to press the 3rd fret on the 1st string.

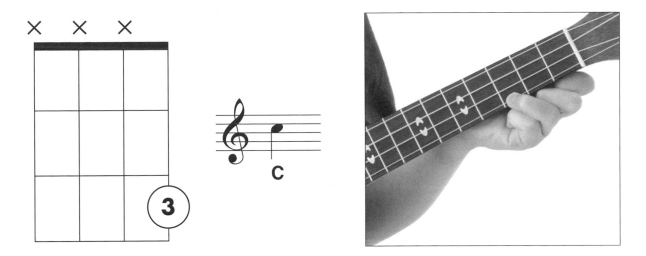

A **half note** (♩) lasts twice as long as a quarter note; it gets two beats.

SEASICK

Count: 1 - 2   3   4

TEACHER ACCOMPANIMENT:

STAIRCLIMBLING

TEACHER ACCOMPANIMENT:

THE NOTE E

Now let's move on to the 2nd string. To play the note E, pluck the 2nd string open.

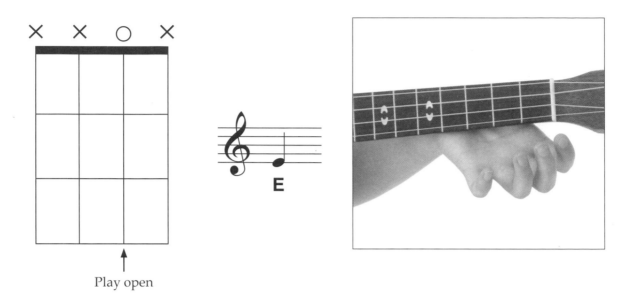

Play open

E

A **whole note** (o) is twice as long as a half note or four times as long as a quarter note. It lasts four beats, or a whole measure in 4/4 time.

THE UKE BLUES 🔊

Count: 1 2 3 4   1 - 2 - 3 - 4

TEACHER ACCOMPANIMENT:

C7

F7

C7   G7   F7   C7

THE NOTE F

Use your 1st finger to press the 2nd string at the 1st fret.

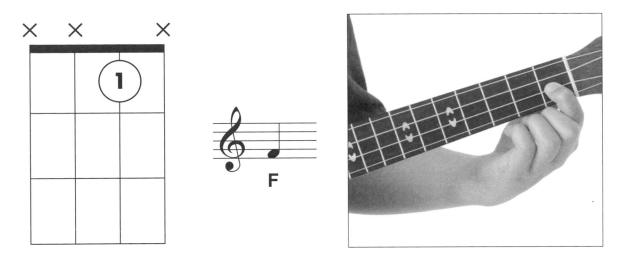

Rests are beats of silence. The **quarter note rest** (𝄽) means to be silent for one beat. Try counting silently when you see a rest.

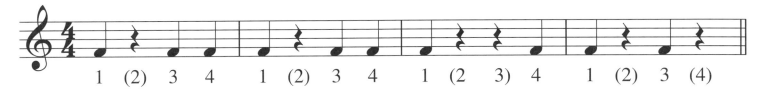

1 (2) 3 4   1 (2) 3 4   1 (2) (3) 4   1 (2) 3 (4)

STOP AND GO 🔊

TEACHER ACCOMPANIMENT:

THE NOTE G

Use your 3rd finger to press the 2nd string at the 3rd fret.

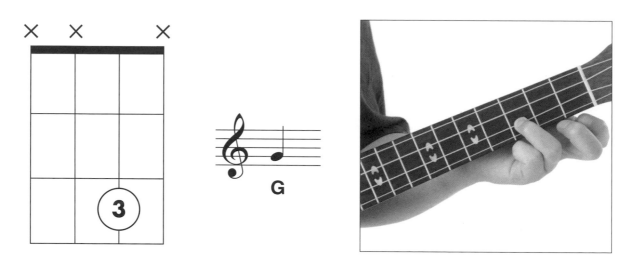

G

A **half note rest** (➖) means to be silent for two beats.

HILL CLIMBING

TEACHER ACCOMPANIMENT:

Try this example with half note rests and quarter note rests. Remember to count!

1   (2)   3   4   1   2   (3)   (4)   1   2   3   (4)   1   (2)   3   4

NOTE REVIEW

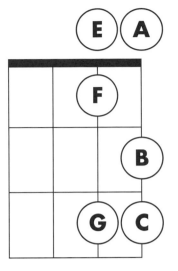

E   F   G   A   B   C

The notes in the following exercises move from string to string. As you are playing one note, look ahead to the next and get your fingers in position.

WINDCHIMES

TEACHER ACCOMPANIMENT:

Some songs begin with **pickup notes**. Count the missing beats out loud before you start playing.

ISLAND STREAM

Teacher plays chord symbols

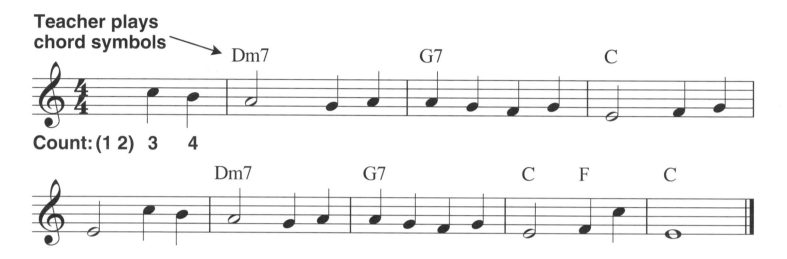

Count: (1 2) 3 4

SHE LOVES YOU

Teacher plays chord symbols

(1)(2)(3) 4
She loves you, yeah, yeah, yeah. She loves you, yeah,

yeah, yeah. She loves you, yeah, yeah, yeah, yeah.

Words and Music by John Lennon and Paul McCartney
Copyright © 1963 by NORTHERN SONGS LIMITED
Copyright Renewed
All rights for the U.S.A., its territories and possessions and Canada assigned to and controlled by GIL MUSIC CORP., 1650 Broadway, New York, NY 10019
International Copyright Secured   All Rights Reserved

THE B♭ CHORD

For the B♭ chord, you'll need to press down all four strings. Lay your 1st finger down across both the 1st and 2nd strings.

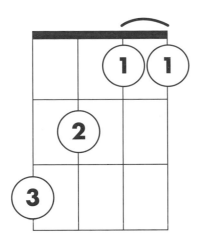

Strum marks are sometimes written on the staff to help you keep track of where the strums are within the measure.

THIS LAND IS YOUR LAND

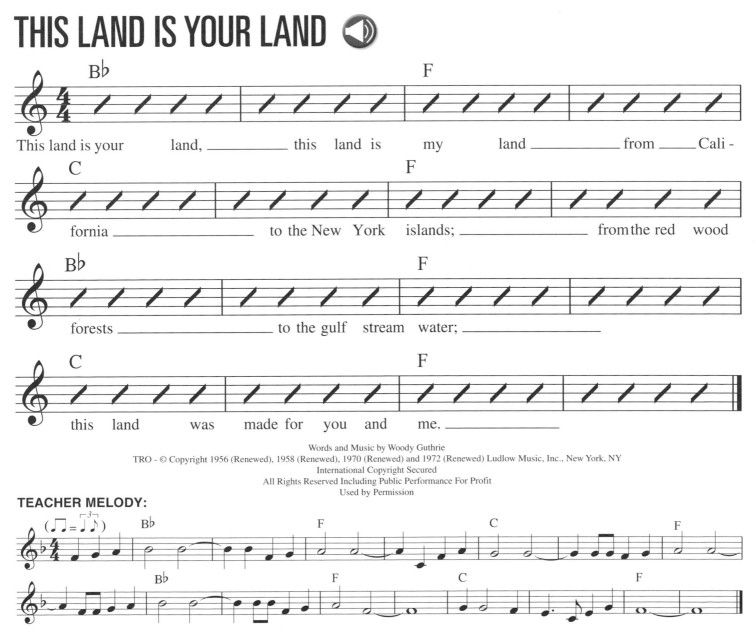

This land is your land, _____ this land is my land _____ from _____ Cali-

fornia _____ to the New York islands; _____ from the red wood

forests _____ to the gulf stream water; _____

this land was made for you and me. _____

TEACHER MELODY:

A **whole note rest** (━) means to be silent for four beats, or a whole measure.

BARBARA ANN

Intro

Ba, Ba, Ba, Ba,   Barbara   Ann.   Ba, Ba, Ba, Ba,   Barbara   Ann. Barbara

Ann,   take   my   hand.   Barbara

Ann,   you   got   me   rockin'   and   a   rollin', rockin'

and   a   reelin'   Barbara   Ann.

Words and Music by Fred Fassert
© 1959 (Renewed 1987) EMI LONGITUDE MUSIC and COUSINS MUSIC INC.
All Rights Controlled and Administered by EMI LONGITUDE MUSIC
All Rights Reserved   International Copyright Secured   Used by Permission

TEACHER MELODY:

So far, you have played four downstrokes for each measure. Now let's strum twice for every beat, or eight times for each measure. Alternate between downstrums and upstrums.

down up down up down up down up

MR. TAMBOURINE MAN

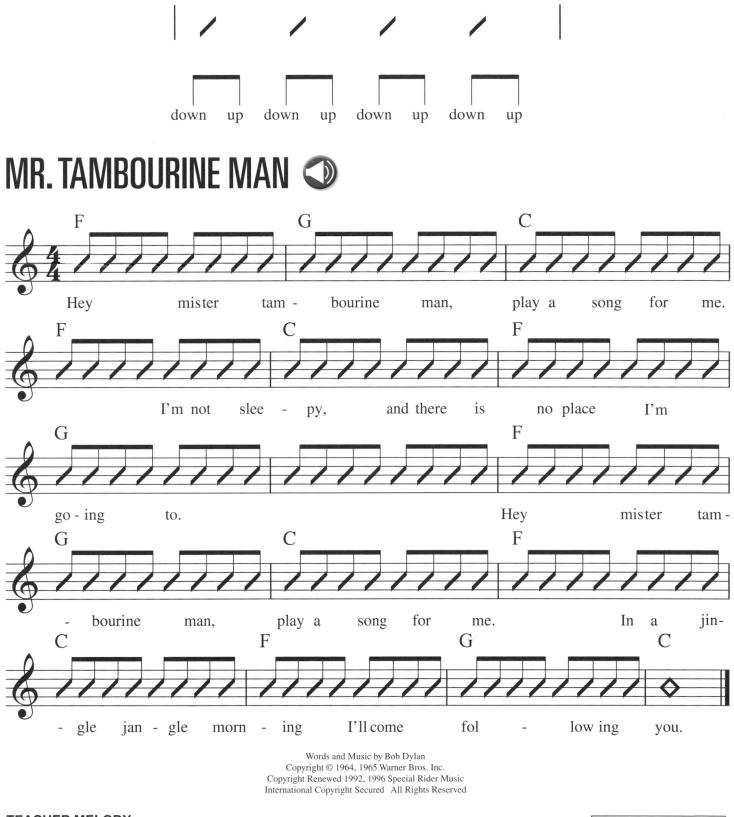

Hey mister tam - bourine man, play a song for me.

I'm not slee - py, and there is no place I'm

go - ing to. Hey mister tam-

- bourine man, play a song for me. In a jin-

- gle jan - gle morn - ing I'll come fol - low ing you.

Words and Music by Bob Dylan
Copyright © 1964, 1965 Warner Bros. Inc.
Copyright Renewed 1992, 1996 Special Rider Music
International Copyright Secured   All Rights Reserved

TEACHER MELODY:

THE NOTES C & D

You already learned how to play the note C on the 1st string. Another (lower) C note can be played by plucking the 3rd string open. To play the D note, press the 3rd string at the 2nd fret.

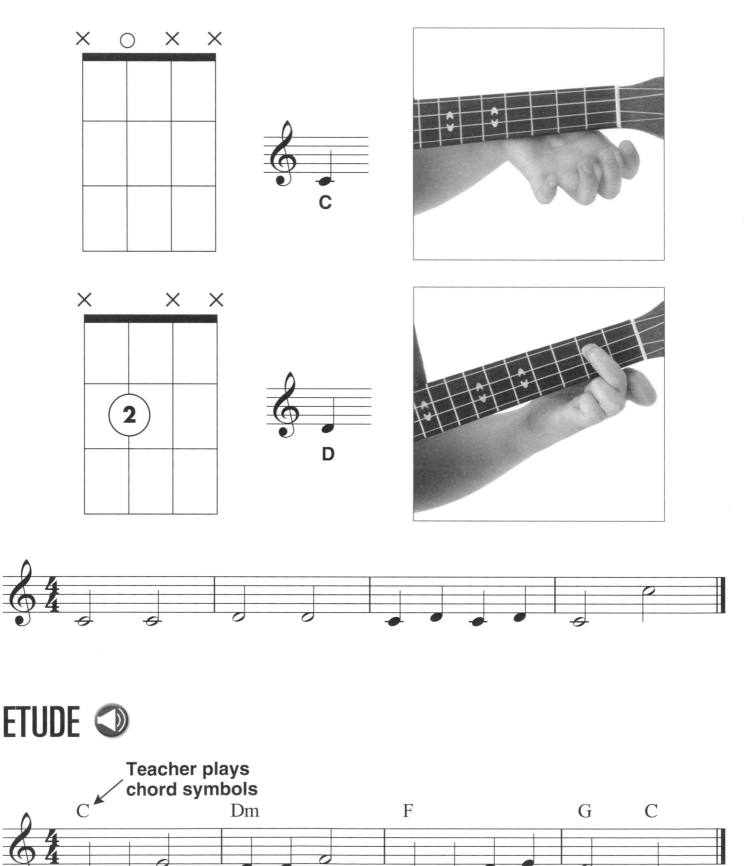

ETUDE

Teacher plays chord symbols

C   Dm   F   G   C

THREE-FOUR TIME

Some music has three beats per measure instead of four. The symbol for three-four time is:

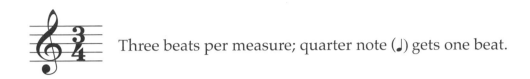

Three beats per measure; quarter note (♩) gets one beat.

AMAZING GRACE

Teacher plays chord symbols

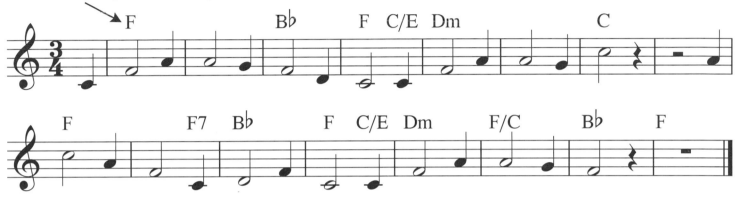

THE NOTE B♭

We have one more note we'll learn. Use your 1st finger to press the 1st string at the 1st fret.

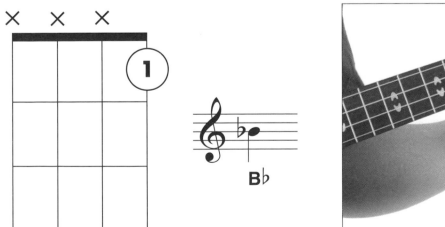

BIRTHDAY SONG

Teacher plays chord symbols

LOVE ME TENDER

Teacher plays chord symbols

Love me ten - der love me sweet; nev - er let me go.

You have made my life com - plete, and I love you so.

Love me ten - der, love me true, all my dreams ful - fill.

For my dar - lin' I love you, and I al - ways will.

Words and Music by Elvis Presley and Vera Matson
Copyright © 1956; Renewed 1984 Elvis Presley Music (BMI)
Worldwide Rights for Elvis Presley Music Administered by BMG Chrysalis
International Copyright Secured   All Rights Reserved

THE SHUFFLE FEEL

Many songs are played with a **shuffle feel**. This means that the eighth notes sound lopsided; the first one in each beat is longer than the second one. The symbol for the shuffle feel is:

Listen to the audio to hear how this sounds on a C chord. First, the chord will be strummed normally; then you'll hear a shuffle feel.

Shuffle Feel

Now try playing "Rock Around the Clock" with a shuffle feel.

ROCK AROUND THE CLOCK 🔊

Intro

One, two three o'clock, four o'clock rock. Five, six, seven o'clock, eight o'clock rock. Nine, ten, eleven o'clock, twelve o'clock rock. We're gonna

Verse

rock a-round the clock tonight. Put your glad rags on and join me hon. We'll have some fun when the clock strikes one. We're gonna rock around the clock tonight. We're gonna rock, rock, rock, 'til the broad daylight. We're gonna rock, gonna rock a-round the clock tonight.

TEACHER MELODY:

etc.

THE G MINOR CHORD

Let's learn one more chord. For the G minor chord, you'll need to press three strings at the same time.

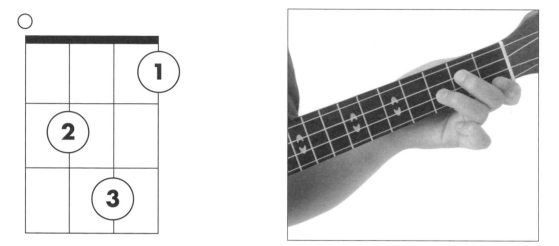

Practice alternating the G minor chord with the other chords you've learned, and then try it out in our last song: "Surfer Girl."

SURFER GIRL

Written by Brian Wilson
© 1962 (Renewed 1990) GUILD MUSIC COMPANY (BMI)/Administered by BUG MUSIC
All Rights Reserved   Used by Permission

CERTIFICATE OF ACHIEVEMENT

Congratulations to

_____
(YOUR NAME)

_____
(DATE)

You have completed

UKULELE FOR KIDS

_____
(TEACHER SIGNATURE)

You are now ready for

HAL LEONARD UKULELE METHOD BOOK 1

HL00695832